AF573916

Blickensderfer

IMAGES OF THE WEST

RUTHERFORD W. WITTHUS

Foreword by
MARTHA A. SANDWEISS

Library of Congress Cataloging-in-Publication Data

Witthus, Rutherford W., 1942-
Blickensderfer: images of the West.

1. Photography—Southwest, New—Landscapes.
2. Southwest, New—Description and travel—Views.
3. Blickensderfer, Clark, 1882-1962. I. Blickensderfer,
Clark, 1882-1962. II. Title.
TR660.W53 1986 779'.092'4 86-13444
ISBN 0-917895-09-6

First Edition
1 2 3 4 5 6 7 8 9

Printed in the United States of America

ISBN: 0-917895-09-6

The first printing of this edition is limited to 2,000 copies, of which 250 are boxed, numbered, and signed by the author. The numbered copies include a reproduction of A Valley of Enchantment by Clark Blickensderfer not included in the unnumbered copies.

This is number

CONTENTS

FOREWORD

CLARK BLICKENSDERFER exemplified the successful pictorial photographer of the 1920s. A self-taught amateur, for whom photography was an absorbing avocation, he exhibited prints in this country and in Europe and earned considerable acclaim in his home town of Denver. As a regional vice-president of the Pictorial Photographers of America, he was in touch with other photographers and aware of the latest developments in the more active artistic centers of New York and California.

Pictorialism was a style promoted in this country around the turn of the century by Alfred Stieglitz and other photographers who hoped to demonstrate conclusively that photography was not a science but an art. These photographers favored soft-focus lenses and often manipulated their prints in the darkroom in an effort to produce photographs that would be artistic "pictures" on a par with paintings. After Stieglitz's elite Photo-Secession group began to break apart in 1910, and Stieglitz himself began to renounce some of the principles of pictorialism, a group of his former colleagues banded together in 1915 to form the Pictorial Photographers of America. This New York-based organization continued to promote the tenets of pictorialism through publications and touring exhibitions, and warmly welcomed the interest and participation of serious amateur photographers from around the country. In the PPA, Blickensderfer found an outlet for the exhibition of his work and a congenial group of colleagues with whom he could share his interest in photography as a creative art form.

Though the PPA had a broad national membership, few of its members ever came from Colorado. During the 1920s, its most active members from the state were Blickensderfer and Laura Gilpin, a professional photographer from Colorado Springs who had studied in New York with Clarence White, one of the founders of the PPA. During the 1920s, Blickensderfer and Gilpin frequently exhibited in the same photographic salons and, indeed, they often photographed the same subject matter. Both were drawn to Denver's new buildings, the beauty of the Colorado Rockies, the ruined cliff dwellings at Mesa Verde, and the exotic architecture of northern New Mexico's Indian pueblos. While Blickensderfer exhibited his work for only a short time, Gilpin pursued her craft for more than sixty years, eventually establishing herself as one of the foremost chroniclers of the Southwest.

Blickensderfer's career was like that pursued by the more typical PPA member, for whom photography was a hobby rather than a job. He was an "amateur" in the very best sense of the word; a person who practiced photography because that was what he loved. He was lucky to have the time, wherewithal and talent to do it well.

Martha A. Sandweiss
Curator of Photographs
Amon Carter Museum

MOUNTAINS THEMSELVES

MOUNTAINS themselves are plausible. You can look
At the ranges one behind the other folding
Into alien blueness with apparent meaning;
But you'll find you need a bird or something that
An old man said when you start to finish a mountain.

Reprinted from WESTERING
By Thomas Hornsby Ferril

Clark Blickensderfer with his camera on a pack-horse trip.
Photograph by Robert Rockwell, June 1923.

BLICKENSDERFER

CLARK BLICKENSDERFER had two qualities well-suited to the temperament of a photographer. He was a patient man and he was a perfectionist. The powerful Rocky Mountain West was chosen as a subject for landscape. Birds were selected for portraiture. The city of Denver was singled out to express his own quiet moods. Blickensderfer's choice of subjects served him well. His impressionistic art photography was known and respected among international photographic circles in the 1920s.

Clark Blickensderfer was born in Denver, Colorado, on September 17, 1882, the son of Eva and James Clark Blickensderfer. James C. Blickensderfer grew up in Ohio on a farm overlooking Lake Erie and, at the age of eighteen, was graduated from Pennsylvania State College as a civil engineer. He was subsequently hired by his uncle, Jacob Blickensderfer, to work for the Union Pacific Railroad. His cousin, Robert, designed the Georgetown Loop, the historic railroad grade in Georgetown, Colorado, which ingeniously looped back over itself.

In 1875 during childbirth, James Blickensderfer's first wife, Mary J. McHenry, and their only child died.

> *Her husband was very distraught by what he considered to be the poor attention his wife had received. To him childbirth was basically an engineering problem. He ceased his career as a civil engineer and decided to become a doctor. He attended the nearest medical school of any repute — Washington University at St. Louis.*[1]

Returning to Denver in 1880, Dr. Blickensderfer associated as a junior partner with Dr. Frederick J. Bancroft. In 1882, on New Years Day, he married Eva White, to whom a son, Clark Blickensderfer, was

Clark Blickensderfer (right) in his tent by the light of campfire. The identity of the person on the left is unknown. Blickensderfer probably took the photograph using a cable release.

born on September 17, 1882. Their purchase of a house on the corner of Seventeenth and California streets in 1885 proved to be a sound investment.

As the financial district began to encroach on the residential area of downtown Denver, a new home for the family was constructed on Colfax and Pennsylvania avenues in 1891. Dr. Blickensderfer decided to develop an office building on the downtown site which was designed specifically for the needs of physicians. The California Building was completed in 1892. In 1893 came the devaluation of silver and the crash. Although his partners in the enterprise suffered great losses, Dr. Blickensderfer was able to pay the large mortgage on the newly completed building.

Clark Blickensderfer attended the old East High School in downtown Denver and chose to study civil engineering at Columbia University in New York City. Roger Toll, who later became superintendent of Rocky Mountain National Park, was Clark's close friend and fellow classmate at Columbia, where both young men received degrees in 1906.

The Blickensderfers had by this time decided to move away from Colfax Avenue because of the dust on the busy street. The 800 block of Grant Street was owned by Dr. Blickensderfer's patient David Moffat, who was building a grand house on the northeast corner of Eighth and Grant. Moffat offered property on the same block at a favorable price to the Blickensderfers, with the idea of having his doctor close at hand. While the house designed by Marean & Norton was being constructed, Dr. and Mrs. Blickensderfer rented a house in Stamford, Connecticut, to be near their only son. When the residence at 866 Grant Street was completed and their son graduated, the family resumed residence in Denver.

Clark occupied himself with the real estate holdings his father had successfully developed. In 1910, he married Miss Elizabeth Walker. The couple lived at 850 Grant Street in a house designed by Clark Blickensderfer.

During the next few years, Clark fostered his interest in photography. He used the many free hours that his financial position allowed him to explore the medium and the surrounding landscape. Above Estes Park, on property obtained from the MacGregor Ranch, he built a retreat, a small cottage, from which he made frequent

Blickensderfer's White automobile, packed with tripod and equipment, in front of his cabin near Estes Park, Colorado.
Photograph by Robert Rockwell.

photographic trips to Rocky Mountain National Park.

His solitary vision of the Rocky Mountains drew him into the school of photography known as pictorialism. The ability to capture the changing light of both the mountains and the city of Denver encouraged him to pursue the soft-focus, impressionistic moods allowed by the techniques of the pictorialists. As a charter member of the Colorado Mountain Club, he found himself surrounded by magnificent natural settings. Morning light shimmering on the trees, evening light departing from the vast expanses of mountain valleys, glowing waters flowing from his beloved mountains, were all subjects for his camera. This grandeur had been depicted on canvas by Bierstadt and Moran; these moments of solitary splendor were now to be captured on film by Blickensderfer.

Blickensderfer had at his disposal three very simple environments: a darkroom in his Denver home, a darkroom for developing glass plates in his mountain cottage, and the space beneath the focusing cloth covering his 4 x 5 Graflex camera. He had in mind three principles: to create an image of a mood into which a solitary person would wish to enter, to produce a well-engineered photograph, and to suffuse the image with beauty. "I want to be there" was the desired response. Armed with this vision, Blickensderfer entered the realm of the Rocky Mountains, stalked the snowy city of Denver, and patiently observed the habitats of his feathered friends to seize those moments which he treasured.

Blickensderfer printed the majority of his images on chloride and bromide papers. These two popular processes enabled him to infuse the image of the snowy landscape with the softness of the atmosphere and to focus on the habitats of wildlife with clarity. Blickensderfer's first published image was in the Colorado Mountain Club's *Trail and Timberline* in 1915.[2] The photograph, entitled *The Dipper's Pool*, presented Chasm Falls on the Fall River Road in Rocky Mountain National Park. The following year, two images of the Estes Park area were published in *Trail and Timberline*, including a view of Longs Peak from Blickensderfer's cottage[3] (Plate 49).

In 1920, Clark Blickensderfer for the first time exhibited images of birds at the Colorado Mountain Club. His interest in ornithological photography continued for many years, although he exhibited few of these bird portraits outside of Colorado. He and his buddy, Robert Rockwell, spent many days and nights together seeking the elusive birds. Packing Clark's gasoline-powered White automobile with cameras,

Blickensderfer pausing under an aspen tree during a photographic trip. Photograph by Robert Rockwell, June 1923.

lenses, and tripods, they wandered the mountains in search of nesting and feeding habitats. Setting up blinds and mammoth tripods, climbing trees with cameras in hand, and waiting for the right moment to open the lens were activities which both Blickensderfer and Rockwell considered pleasurable. Robert Rockwell was a serious student of ornithology; his works on the birds of the Rocky Mountains are still read avidly.[4]

In 1922, at the instigation of George William Eggers, director of the Denver Art Museum, the Denver Camera Club was founded as an allied group of the museum. "Previous to that time the only Colorado pictorial photographer known internationally was Mr. Clark Blickensderfer, president of the organization."[5] The club's purpose was to develop pictorial photography as an art form in Denver. It met every Wednesday evening at the Chappell House, the headquarters of the Denver Art Museum. Lectures and training in pictorial photography were offered with the goal of presenting images of Denver and the Rocky Mountain region "to the world in its most intriguing aspects."[6] The Denver Camera Club was "open to anyone interested in pictorial photography, upon application and approval."[7] The entire May-June 1925 issue of Denver's *Municipal Facts* was devoted to publishing the photographic works of the club members.

Blickensderfer's renown came as a result of his salon images. In 1923, *Winter Shadows* (Plate 42) was accepted in both the International Exhibition of the London Salon of Photography and the Thirty-second Annual Salon of Photography of the Toronto Camera Club. In the same year, Blickensderfer showed at the International Salon of the Pictorial Photographers of America in New York City. The jury of selection included Alfred Stieglitz and Clarence H. White. The reviewer, W.G. Bowdoin, considered the show "the most important exhibition of photographic prints ever assembled in [New York]."[8] Blickensderfer's co-exhibitors included, among others, Edward Weston and Laura Gilpin. Bowdoin singled out two of Blickensderfer's images:

> *"The Ptarmigan: A Snow Bird of the Rockies" by Clark Blickensderfer of Denver, Col., makes an interesting number. The bird, whose habitat is in the high altitudes of the mountains, changes its plumage four times a year. In the show photograph (a chloride), the feathered one is dressed in winter white against the snow*

Blickensderfer in a tree with his camera patiently waiting to photograph a bird.

background and to show white on white, is some photographic stunt.

The same artist shows "The Union Station" (at Denver), with its diverging tracks showing black on the snow covered ground of the train terminal.[9]

Blickensderfer continued to show in the international salons. *The Union Station* (Plate 36) and other snow scenes around Denver and the mountains were accepted in major shows. By 1925, Blickensderfer was a regional vice-president of the Pictorial Photographers of America. *Turmoil* (Plate 39) was shown in four exhibitions in the United States and Canada. *Winter Shadows* was called a "fine piece of decorative photography" by the reviewers in *American Photography.*[10] The annual competitions held by the magazine included many of Blickensderfer's images. "Clark Blickensderfer continues to work in a high key, his best pictures being *The Union Station*, now well known, and *Winter Above Timberline*, a cold and majestic rendering of snow in the high mountains."[11]

F.C. Tilney, in his review of the First Annual Exhibition of the International Circle of Pictorial Photographers, praised Blickensderfer's handling of snow scenes.

Clark Blickensderfer (Denver), finds inspiration out of doors in his snowy country. His "Ptarmigan, A Snow Bird of the Rockies" is a smart piece of work, not only from the point of view of stalking, but in the delicate adjustment of tones just a single degree removed from white, by which the white bird is perfectly relieved against the snow and has modelling and texture. Whether telephotography has been pressed into service or not I cannot say, but "Winter Above Timberline" is clear and sharp enough to suggest it. Purity and dryness of the air might permit of this crisp and minute detail on the side of distant mountains; but to one who is used to vapor in the air these mountains appear so near as to resemble the view one would get through strong binoculars. The tone values of snow and bare rock are excellently kept. But Mr. Blickensderfer surpasses all in his third landscape, "The Storm is Abroad in the Mountain." Here we have not only

Camp at the end of Fall River Road, Rocky Mountain National Park, Colorado. Blickensderfer is on the left, Alfred Evans on the right.
Photograph by Robert Rockwell, August 21, 1919.

> *technical prowess, but the mood of Nature, and the result is poetry as well as science and art. The design is large in style by reason of its simplicity, and the storm cloud is finely rendered.*[12]

In 1926, Blickensderfer submitted exhibition prints executed in a process known as bromoil. The cold chloride was replaced with the warmth of bromoil. P.F. Squier, reviewing the Thirteenth Annual Pittsburgh Salon of Photographic Art, received the new prints with admiration.

> *. . . we find Blickensderfer in a new field. Gone are his cold, wintry snow pictures, that we have come to associate with his name and in their place we find three bromoils. From the class of his first bromoils we believe he is on the road to greater fame. He achieves great delicacy of feeling in his handling of the light toned building in sunlight in "The Closed Gate" and then rich, full of life tones in his shadows in "Arches of Capistrano." Both of these are real pictures as well as fine bromoils.*[13]

The year 1927 proved to be an outstanding one for Clark Blickensderfer. The Camera Club of New York requested a large number of prints to be sent to them for a one-man show.[14] Blickensderfer gathered together his most important images, including many bird studies, and shipped them to New York. The show was mounted in May 1927. The prints were exhibited in December of the same year at the Chicago Camera Club.

The late 1920s saw the end of Blickensderfer's interest in salon photographs. His new passion was the 4 x 5 color lantern slide. No longer were the mountains depicted in their atmospheric solitude; rather, the sharp, crisp sunlight on the brilliantly colored wild flowers captured Blickensderfer's imagination. Clear days beckoned him to the hills; the stormy, cloudy days of his youth had lost their intrigue.

As Blickensderfer grew older, a new technology, the 35mm camera, aroused his interest, and he began to shoot highly saturated Kodachrome slides. Until a few years before his death in 1962 at the age of seventy-nine, Clark Blickensderfer experimented with the brilliance of projected color slides to recreate Colorado's glowing sunrises and the intense hues of mountain wild flowers.

END NOTES

1. J.C. Blickensderfer, II, *The Life of Dr. James Clark Blickensderfer* (Denver, Colorado: Unpublished manuscript, 1970), p. 4.

2. Colorado Mountain Club, *Trail and Timberline, An Annual Mountaineering Review in Pictures*, 1915.

3. Colorado Mountain Club, *Trail and Timberline, An Annual Mountaineering Review in Pictures*, 1916.

4. Robert Niedrock and Robert Rockwell, *Birds of Denver and Mountain Parks* (Denver, Colorado: Colorado Museum of Natural History, 1939).

5. "The Denver Camera Club Number," *Municipal Facts*, Volume VII, Numbers 5-6, May-June 1925, p. 13.

6. *Ibid.*

7. *Ibid.*

8. W.G. Bowdoin, "International Camera Salon at The Art Centre," *The Evening World*, May 29, 1923.

9. *Ibid.*

10. "Our Illustrations," *American Photography*, Volume XIX, Number 1, January 1925, p. 59.

11. F.R. Fraprie, "Some Spring Picture Shows—Buffalo," *American Photography*, Volume XIX, Number 5, May 1925, p. 246.

12. F.C. Tilney, "American Work at the First Annual Exhibition of the International Pictorial Photographers," *American Photography*, Volume XIX, Number 7, July 1925, p. 372.

13. P.F. Squier, "The Thirteenth Pittsburgh Salon," *American Photography*, Volume XX, Number 7, July 1926, pp. 341-342.

14. Martin Heidegger, *Poetry, Language, Thought*, translation and introduction by Albert Hofstadter (New York: Harper & Row, 1971), p. 7.

PLATES

Plate 1: The Approaching Storm

Plate 2: A Sunlight Decoration

Plate 3: Black Canyon

Plate 4: Curves and Ripples

Plate 5: Through the Window

Plate 6: Homeward Bound

Plate 7: Navajo Canyon

Plate 8: Round Tower, Cliff Palace

Plate 9: Twilight, Mesa Verde

Plate 10: Loafing

Plate 11: Lines and Angles

Plate 12: San Ildefonso

Plate 13: The Wood Peddler

Plate 14: Indian Pueblo

Plate 15: Evening Fishing

Plate 16: Old Faithful

Plate 17: Half Dome

Plate 18: Yosemite Falls

Plate 19: The Grand Canyon

Plate 20: At San Fernando

Plate 21: Feeding the Chickens

Plate 22: Arches of Capistrano

Plate 23: A Portal of the Past

Plate 24: At Ebb-tide

Plate 25: The Dancing Girl

Plate 26: 1600 Logan Street

Plate 27: The Closed Gate

Plate 28: Snow and Marble

Plate 29: The Deserted Bench

Plate 30: Woman with the Umbrella

Plate 31: The Path of Gold

Plate 32: When Winter Comes

Plate 33: City Smoke

Plate 34: Commerce

Plate 35: Industry

Plate 36: The Union Station

Plate 37: Winter Coral

Plate 38: Gray Dawn

Plate 39: Turmoil

Plate 40: Twilight in the Rockies

Plate 41: Winter Above Timberline

Plate 42: Winter Shadows

Plate 43: The Approaching Storm

Plate 44: An Intriguing Trail

Plate 45: Evening at Timberline

Plate 46: Evening, Estes Park

Plate 47: Path of Light

Plate 48: Harp of the North

Plate 49: From My Cottage Window

Plate 50: Silence

Plate 51: Ptarmigan, the Snow Bird of the Rockies

Plate 52: Southern White-tailed Ptarmigan, Summer Plumage

Plate 53: Western Horned Owl Brooding Young on Nest

Plate 54: Young Western Horned Owls

Plate 55: Young Western Horned Owls

Plate 56: Adult Screech Owl

Plate 57: Adult Saw-whet Owl Looking out of Nest

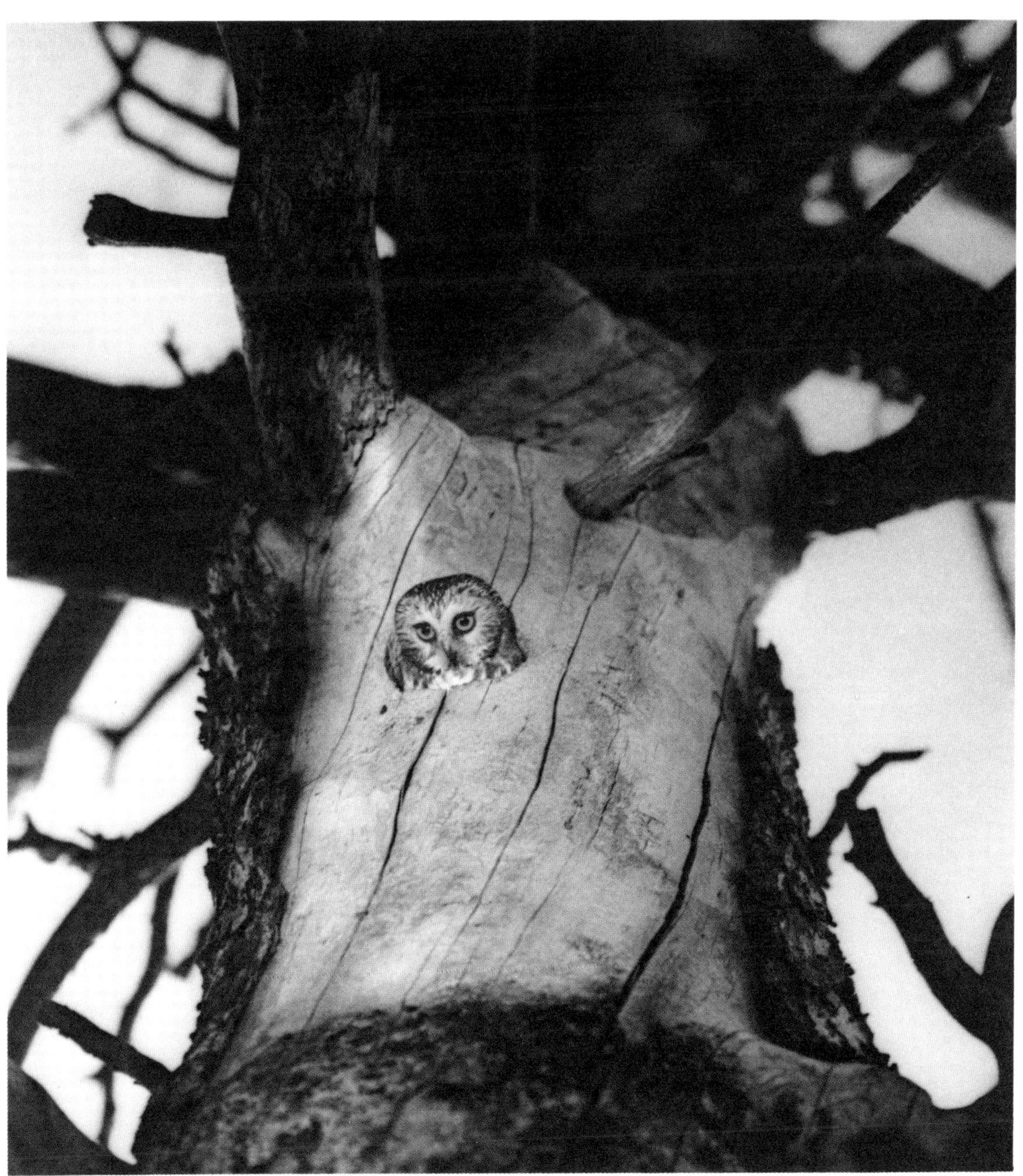

Plate 58: Barn Owl on Nest (15-minute exposure)

Plate 59: Young Barn Owl Family

Plate 60: Adult Roadrunner and Young

Plate 61: Roadrunner's Nest, Young, and Egg

Plate 62: Western Flycatcher

Plate 63: Adult Black-chinned Hummingbird

Plate 64: Barn Owl

LIST OF PLATES

Plate 21: Feeding the Chickens
33 x 26 cm.
Japanese Tea Garden, Golden Gate Park, San Francisco, California

Plate 22: Arches of Capistrano
33 x 26 cm.

Plate 23: A Portal of the Past
26 x 31 cm.
Palace of the Legion of Honor, San Francisco

Plate 24: At Ebb Tide
23 x 33 cm.

Plate 25: The Dancing Girl
26 x 19 cm.

Plate 26: 1600 Logan Street
29 x 24 cm.
William G. Fisher residence (now Claus Heppner & Associates)

Plate 27: The Closed Gate
32 x 26 cm.
Cathedral High School, 1824 Logan Street, Denver

Plate 28: Snow and Marble
33 x 25 cm.
Doric colonnade of the United States Post Office and Federal Court

Plate 29: The Deserted Bench
31 x 25 cm.
Cheesman Park, Denver

Plate 30: Woman with the Umbrella
26 x 23 cm.
Colorado state capitol

Plate 31: The Path of Gold
27 x 22 cm.
Voorhies Memorial at Christmas, Denver

Plate 32: When Winter Comes
23 x 31 cm.
Denver Country Club

Plate 33: City Smoke
28 x 23 cm.
Denver, Colorado

Plate 34: Commerce
Daniels and Fisher Tower, Denver, seen through a heavy snowstorm

Plate 35: Industry
25 x 32 cm.
Denver's Union Terminal freight yards

Plate 36: The Union Station
32 x 25 cm.
Denver's Union Station

Plate 37: Winter Coral
26 x 25 cm.
Cheesman Memorial, Cheesman Park, Denver

Plate 38: Gray Dawn
32 x 26 cm.
Yellow pine

Plate 39: Turmoil
25 x 32 cm.
Glacier Gorge, Rocky Mountain National Park

Plate 40: Twilight in the Rockies
25 x 32 cm.

Plate 41: Winter Above Timberline
29 x 26 cm.

Plate 42: Winter Shadows
23 x 32 cm.

Plate 43: The Approaching Storm
24 x 32 cm.

Plate 44: An Intriguing Trail
31 x 23 cm.
Fall River Road,
Rocky Mountain National Park

Plate 45: Evening at Timber Line
31 x 25 cm.

Plate 46: Evening, Estes Park
19 x 29 cm.
Estes Park and the Mummy Range from
Park Hill on the Lyons Road

Plate 47: Path of Light
28 x 23 cm.

Plate 48: Harp of the North
24 x 32 cm.

Plate 49: From My Cottage Window
24 x 31 cm.
Longs Peak from Blickensderfer's cabin

Plate 50: Silence
28 x 24 cm.

Plate 51: Ptarmigan: Snow Bird of the Rockies
29 x 26 cm.

Plate 52: Southern White-Tailed Ptarmigan, Summer Plumage
19 x 24 cm.

Plate 53: Western Horned Owl Brooding Young on Nest
21 x 27 cm.

Plate 54: Young Western Horned Owls
23 x 28 cm.

Plate 55: Young Western Horned Owls
18 x 24 cm.

Plate 56: Adult Screech Owl
22 x 19 cm.

Plate 57: Adult Saw-whet Owl Looking out of Nest
28 x 23 cm.

Plate 58: Barn Owl on Nest (15-minute exposure)
21 x 29 cm.

Plate 59: Young Barn Owl Family
13 x 26 cm.

Plate 60: Adult Roadrunner and Young
21 x 27 cm.

Plate 61: Roadrunner's Nest, Young, and Egg
19 x 24 cm.

Plate 62: Western Flycatcher
24 x 19 cm.

Plate 63: Adult Black-chinned Hummirgbird
24 x 19 cm.

Plate 64: Barn Owl
28 x 24 cm.

Exhibition by Clark Blickensderfer, California Camera Club, San Francisco, California, November 15 to December 15, 1924.

LIST OF SHOWS

1920

3rd Annual Colorado Mountain Club
Photographic Exhibit
(May 18-31, 1920)
A Gentleman Thief (Long Crested Jay)
The Tramp (Camp Bird)
Chasm Falls (Fall River Road, Estes Park)
Above the Clouds (Long's Peak)
Who Goes There? (Mule deer, doe)
The Serpent

1923

International Exhibition of the
London Salon of Photography
A Ptarmigan in Winter
Winter Shadows

Thirty-second Annual Salon of Photography
of the Toronto Camera Club
(Canadian National Exhibition)
(August 25-September 8, 1923)
Evening at Timberline (Plate 45)
At San Fernando (Plate 20)
At Ebb Tide (Plate 24)
Ptarmigan
Winter Shadows (Plate 42)

6th Annual Colorado Mountain Club
Photographic Exhibit
(May 7-19, 1923)
The Union Station (Plate 36)
Open Water on the Trail to Fern Lake
Ptarmigan
Rocky Mountain Jay
The Limber Pine

1924

Eleventh Annual Pittsburgh Salon
of Photographic Art
(March 2-31, 1924)
The Union Station (Plate 36)
Winter above Timberline (Plate 41)
Industry (Plate 35)
Winter Shadows (Plate 42)

Third Annual International Exhibition
of Pictorial Photography,
Pictorial Photographic Society of
San Francisco
(October 31-December 7, 1924)
The Union Station (Plate 36)
Industry (Plate 35)
Winter above Timberline (Plate 41)

Thirty-third Annual Salon of the
Toronto Club
(Canadian National Exhibition)
(August 23-September 6, 1924)
The Storm Is Abroad in the Mountains
A Portal of the Past (Plate 23)
City Smoke (Plate 33)

7th Annual Colorado Mountain Club
Photographic Exhibit
(May 12-24, 1924)
"It Blew and Friz and Snew Again"
Winter above Timberline (Plate 41)

A Wet Day
Snow and Marble (Plate 28)

1925

Buffalo Salon (Buffalo Camera Club)
Industry (Plate 35)
Turmoil (Plate 39)

Denver Camera Club Annual Exhibition
Twilight in the Rockies (Plate 40)

Pictorial Photographers of America, New York
(March 1925)
The Snow
Winter Shadows (Plate 42)
Storm
Turmoil (Plate 39)
At Ebb Tide (Plate 24)
A Valley of Enchantment

Salon International de Photographie, Paris
(October 1925)
Winter Shadows (Plate 42)

Third Annual Salon of the Southwest Museum
Southern California Camera Club, Los Angeles, California
The Deserted Bench (Plate 29)

Thirty-fourth Annual Salon of the Toronto Camera Club
(Canadian National Exhibition)
(August 29-September 12, 1925)
A Winter Morning
Evening Fishing (Plate 15)
Gray Dawn (Plate 38)

8th Annual Colorado Mountain Club Photographic Exhibit
(May 4-16, 1925)
Turmoil (Plate 39)
The Beginning of Winter
Storm
Blue and Silver
Twilight in the Rockies (Plate 40)
From My Cottage Window (Plate 49)
A Winter Morning

Second International Salon of Pictorial Photography,
Pictorial Photographers of America, New York
(May 19-June 15, 1925)
Winter above Timberline (Plate 41)
Turmoil (Plate 39)

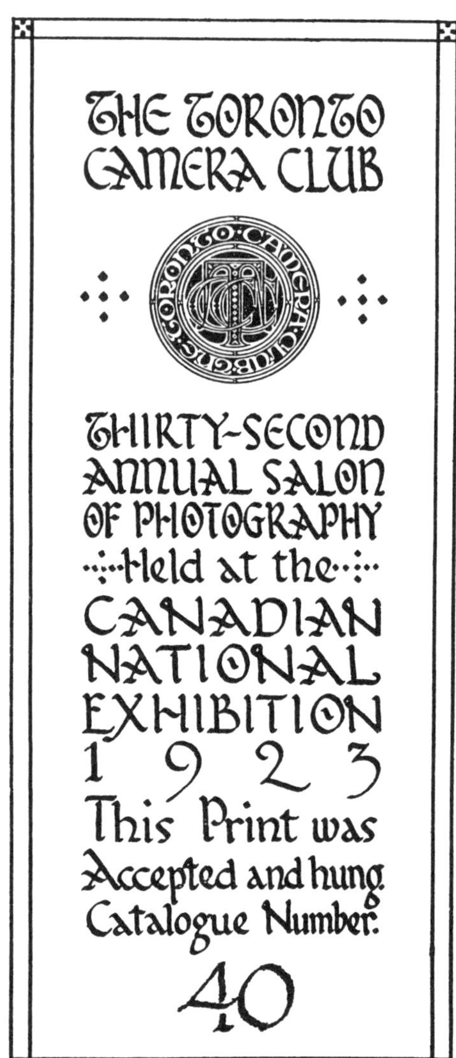

1926

Thirteenth Annual Pittsburgh Salon of Photographic Art
(March 14-April 18, 1926)
Roofs and Chimneys
Arches of Capistrano (Plate 22)
The Closed Gate (Plate 27)

Fourth International Exhibition of Pictorial Photography,
Pictorial Photographic Society of San Francisco
(October 17-31, 1926)
Winter Shadows (Plate 42)
The Silver Dome

Fifth Annual Western Salon of Pictorial Photography,
Southern California Camera Club,
Los Angeles, California
(November 15-30, 1926)
Industry (Plate 35)
Gray Dawn (Plate 38)
Lines and Angles (Plate 11)

1927

The Camera Club, New York
(May 1927)
Snow and Marble (Plate 28)
Winter Morning
The Silver Dome
The City
1600 Logan Street (Plate 26)
Winter Coral (Plate 37)
When Winter Comes (Plate 32)
A Winter Walk
The Deserted Bench (Plate 29)
From My Cottage Window (Plate 49)
An Intriguing Trail (Plate 44)
Twilight in the Rockies (Plate 40)
Path of Light (Plate 47)
Harp of the North (Plate 48)
Evening at Timber Line (Plate 45)
The Approaching Storm (Plate 1)
The Storm Is Abroad in the Mountains
Storm
Breath of Boreas
Turmoil (Plate 39)
Adult Saw-whet Owl Looking Out of Nest (Plate 57)
Young Saw-whet Owls
Barn Owl on Nest (15-minute exposure) (Plate 58)

Young Barn Owl Family (Plate 59)
Barn Owl (Plate 64)
Long-eared Owl
Western Horned Owl Brooding Young on Nest
Violet-green Swallow
Ptarmigan, Snow Bird of the Rockies (Plate 51)
Sand Mountains
Twilight, Mesa Verde (Plate 9)
San Ildefonso (Plate 12)
Loafing (Plate 10)
Old Faithful (Plate 16)
The Shore Line
Half Dome (Plate 17)
Homeward Bound (Plate 6)
The Weeping Willow
The Dancing Girl (Plate 25)

Special Exhibition, Chicago Camera Club (December 1927)
Snow and Marble (Plate 28)
Winter Morning
The Silver Dome
When Winter Comes (Plate 32)
From My Cottage Window (Plate 49)
An Intriguing Trail (Plate 44)
Twilight in the Rockies (Plate 40)
Path of Light (Plate 47)
Harp of the North (Plate 48)
Evening at Timberline (Plate 45)
The Storm Is Abroad in the Mountains
Breath of Boreas
Turmoil (Plate 39)
The Shore Line
Homeward Bound (Plate 6)

18th ANNUAL PHOTOGRAPHIC EXHIBITION

1935

1928

The Camera Club, New York (September 1928)
Adult Black-chinned Hummingbird (Plate 63)

1929

6th Annual Exhibition of the Denver Camera Club (March 16-31, 1929)
Western Horned Owl Brooding Young on Nest (Plate 53)
Young California Shrike
Violet-green Swallow
White-tailed Ptarmigan in Winter

Omaha Camera Club (February 14, 1929)
Winter Shadows (Plate 42)
Turmoil (Plate 39)
Adult Black-chinned Hummingbird (Plate 63)

1931

Fourteenth Annual Colorado Mountain Club Photographic Exhibition
Sand Dunes
The Sentinel

1935

Eighteenth Annual Colorado Mountain Club Photographic Exhibition
Gray Dawn (Plate 38)
The Approaching Storm (Plate 1)
Sand Waves
Sand Mountains
Navajo Canyon (Plate 7)

ACKNOWLEDGEMENTS

For more than a year, it has been my pleasure to be the caretaker of a collection of superb photographs by Clark Blickensderfer. Friends and family have viewed the hundreds of images and negatives of this Colorado photographer and have helped me select those which appear in this publication.

To Betsy Ashe, Blickensderfer's daughter, and her husband, Dr. S.M. Prather Ashe, go many thanks for their encouragement and help in supplying the photographs and negatives, without which this book would not be possible. They provided me the opportunity to see Blickensderfer's mountain cottage and darkroom, carefully unaltered over the years, and have been very patient with my innumerable questions. Mr. James Clark Blickensderfer kindly allowed me to sort through his father's prints, offering his entire collection for use in this book. His excellent biography of Dr. James Clark Blickensderfer offered many insights into the family's history. Mrs. Catherine Yeager read the biography of her father and gave helpful advice.

While in Fort Worth, Texas, on a study trip to the Amon Carter Museum, to view the Laura Gilpin images of Denver architecture by Fisher & Fisher, I had the pleasure of working with Marni Sandweiss, who added support to this project by mentioning Laura Gilpin's admiration for Blickensderfer's photography. Her foreword adds immeasurably to this book. Milan Hughston, Associate Librarian of the Amon Carter Museum, provided valuable assistance by sharing his research of early twentieth-century salon photography.

Bruce and Virginia Rockwell allowed me to print the negatives of Robert Rockwell, Blickensderfer's photographic companion and fellow bird-lover. For us to see the photographer at work is due to their kind assistance.

The Denver photographer Ronald W. Wohlauer previewed the collection of prints and offered helpful insights. Liz Clancy and Kristine Haglund guided me through the collection of Blickensderfer negatives of birds at the Denver Museum of Natural History. Melissa Bradley was instrumental in locating periodical reviews of photographic exhibitions. Eleanor Gehres and Augie Mastrogiuseppe have worked with me to secure the donation of the negatives to the Western History Department of the Denver Public Library.

Jay Schafer deserves my gratitude for his editing skills, his clarity of vision, his constant enthusiasm, and his endless patience. He sees more than most.

Rutherford W. Witthus
April 1986

BLICKENSDERFER: *Images of the West was designed and typeset in Goudy Oldstyle by Dianne Borneman of Shadow Canyon Graphics, Evergreen, Colorado, and was printed on Mohawk Superfine paper by Arcata Graphics of Kingsport, Tennessee. The dust jacket was designed by Robert Schram of Book Ends, Boulder, Colorado.*